OIL PASTELS

Jacqueline Black

HarperCollins*Publishers*

First published in 1993
by HarperCollins Publishers
London

© Jacqueline Black, 1993

Editor: Patsy North
Art Editor: Caroline Hill
Layout: Tim Higgins
Photographer: Ed Barber

Photographs of the author on pages 4 and 5 courtesy of
IPC Magazines Ltd 1991/Robert Harding Syndication

The author asserts the moral right to be
identified as the author of this work.

A catalogue record for this book is available from the British Library

ISBN 0 00 412635 1

Printed and bound in Hong Kong

CONTENTS

PORTRAIT OF AN ARTIST
JACQUELINE BLACK

Fig. 1 Jacqueline Black in her studio

Jacqueline Black was born in Brighton and now lives in South-West France, where over the last fifteen years she has painted and has also established La Delmazou Summer Painting School.

As a child aged seven, she started a collection of poster paint colours in glass jars and, exhilarated by the intensity of the colours, she determined to be a painter. During her early childhood she enjoyed the atmosphere of Hampstead, in London, before an exciting period on a houseboat in Chiswick Mall. She then studied for four years at St Martin's College of Art, London, whose traditional methods of teaching essential skills and techniques instilled in her a continuing respect and love for working in a wide range of media. Jacqueline has always felt compelled to use colour and design as a means of expressing visually her personal response to her immediate surroundings.

Over the years, whilst working primarily as a freelance artist, Jacqueline Black's career has benefited from the experience and breadth of working as a consultant designer, an illustrator at Oxford University Press, a Welfare artist, and most importantly, as a teacher. Her enthusiasm combined with her firm grounding in technique have developed the pleasure, interest and skills of many painters and achieved excellent results over the years. She went on to become an Examiner for the Oxford and Cambridge Joint Board before moving to France with her family and later to establish Le Delmazou.

Jacqueline Black's considerable experience and ability to teach technique soon established Le Delmazou as one of the most respected and written about Summer Painting Schools in Europe – enthusiastic articles in *The Guardian* and *The Times*, as well as in magazines such as *Woman's Journal*, *Homes & Gardens* and *Decoration-Schöner Wohnen*, have been complemented by interviews on radio and television. In addition, Jacqueline Black writes for *The Artist* and *Leisure Painter* magazines. She is a regular exhibitor in London galleries, has shown at the Royal Academy Summer Exhibition and exhibits her work in France. Her paintings are in many private collections as well as being sought and distributed worldwide through reproduction as posters and cards. She is also a member of the Women Artists Slide Library.

Since moving to France she has worked more and more in pastels, inspired by the brilliance of the landscape surrounding her home, the sunflowers, poppies, vines and rich choice of local fruits. Likewise domestic objects particular to the region, discovered in local shops and markets, have become a feature of the old French farmhouse where she lives and are a recurrent motif in her work. Working with pastels, both oil and soft, enhances the decorative qualities in her choice of subject and form, producing a feeling of excitement and light which she finds particularly characteristic of this medium.

Recognition of Jacqueline Black's work in France led to her election in 1989 as President of L'Association France-Grande-Bretagne (Tarn), an organisation formed to promote the exchange of artistic and cultural ideas and activities between France and England.

Fig. 2 Jacqueline Black painting in the fields near her home in France

OIL PASTELS
A DIFFERENT MEDIUM

Fig. 3 *Red Apples*

I am happy to say that as a result of using oil pastels over the last few years, and in particular as a result of producing work for this book, I have grown to appreciate the seemingly endless effects that can be achieved with this imaginative and liberating medium. Are you thinking of trying oil pastels? As yet they are not commonly used and few people are aware of their potential as an expressive and creative medium.

The range of colours, which is growing ever larger, now offers a considerable choice. The original colour range was fairly limited, but it is now possible to choose from a wide selection of beautiful clear colours, from soft pale shades through to the richest and most vibrant of hues. This variety of colours allows for pictorial imagery in which there can be, in one painting, both quiet, delicate passages and, by contrast, brilliantly coloured and luminous areas.

Combined with this versatility is the fact that oil pastels do not necessarily require any colour mixing or the use of mixing agents, and need no more than a sheet of ordinary white paper as a support. This makes them amongst the most spontaneous of artists' colours.

Together with the robust nature of the coloured sticks, these qualities enable the artist to work at home or outdoors with great freedom, excitement and pleasure. It is also worth noting that the initial financial outlay to establish your collection need not be considerable.

As you will discover further on in the book, oil pastels also mix easily with other media, encouraging the use of a broad range of textural experimentation, as their tactile quality inspires one to invent different surfaces while work is in progress. However, it is not only with these more modern techniques that oil pastels show their great potential. You can also achieve effects and images which are more commonly associated with the better-known traditional artists' colours. In other words it is possible to extend your style and technique in many different directions, from known to unknown methods, discovering for yourself the satisfaction of a fresh and new visual vocabulary.

These are just some of the characteristics that I find so enjoyable when using oil pastels and that have led me to describe them as both a different and dynamic medium for the amateur and professional artist alike.

Fig. 4 *Repeating Image*

WHAT EQUIPMENT DO YOU NEED?

Fig. 5 A personal selection of oil pastels in a variety of makes and colours

A box of oil pastels, almost any paper or card support to work on, a knife or blade for engraving to remove layers of colour and, when appropriate, to sharpen the pastels – these are your basic requirements to begin exploring the energetic and colourful characteristics of this medium.

Oil pastels

Choosing oil pastels from the growing range available in the shops is fun, but can be confusing. In general, the colour descriptions given to artists' paints are consistent, but at present the colour description given to oil pastels varies from one manufacturer to another. Some

offer numbers only, others number and colour names, and quite often the colour name will be inadequate.

For instance, a yellow that would normally be described as a chrome yellow could, in an oil pastel range, be called Yellow/No.3. In order to make the colour descriptions clearer in this book, I have used general terms that apply most commonly to all artists' colours. So in the case of the Yellow/No.3, I have called it chrome yellow, which is the true colour description. Although oil pastels are wrapped in paper to protect them and make them less sticky to handle, there is always enough of the coloured stick showing for easy identification. Even if you are not familiar with the traditional colour descriptions given to paints, you will have no difficulty in selecting suitable oil pastel colours as you require them.

If you are fortunate enough to live near a supplier which sells the pastel sticks individually, I suggest that you start buying just a small number of colours. There are considerable variations in the general qualities and covering power of different makes of oil pastel, so it is preferable to avoid committing yourself to a large number at this stage. If you do have to buy a boxed collection, begin by buying the smallest quantity that you can.

When you have a selection of several different makes of oil pastel to experiment with, you will discover that some pastels are softer and some harder than others, and there are those that can be described as being chalkier and others that feel waxier. These variations in texture are produced by the different proportions of materials used in the binding processes – the waxes, tallows, linseed oils etc.

Do not be daunted by the choice of oil pastels available. The range is not enormous and you will soon discover which pastels suit you best. Perhaps, like me, you will end up with a personal collection of several different makes as shown in **fig. 5**, some chosen for their particular covering power and others for their range of colours. As your experience and confidence increase, you might find yourself buying some of the giant-size sticks. As their description implies, these are much larger than the standard ranges and are mainly used for covering large areas.

Containers

Most boxes containing oil pastels are strong and rigid and will protect your pastels well, but some collections come in cardboard containers which tend to become rather shabby with use. In this case, find a flat tin or wooden box to replace the original one. You will need a good box or two, anyway, if you begin to collect your own individual sticks. Always put a sheet of corrugated cardboard in the box to 'bed' the pastels down, and find a piece of soft cloth or plastic foam to place on top to prevent movement, and therefore breakages.

A work tray In order to give myself maximum freedom when working, I like to have a tray to hand in which I can lay out my pastels. If you do not have a suitable tray at home, it is very easy to make one like the example shown in **fig. 6**. You will need:

- a piece of plywood measuring approximately 41 × 55 cm (16 × 22 in)
- a length of batten 1.5 cm (½ in) wide and 192 cm (76 in) long
- panel pins
- wood glue

Cut the batten to fit the sides and ends of the plywood base, then glue and pin the cut battens around the edges.

This tray is as useful indoors as it is outdoors. As you work, your empty tray will gradually fill up with the colours you select for the picture in progress, allowing you to find your working colours easily and giving you

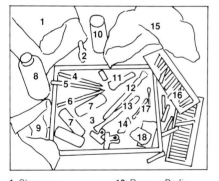

1 Clean rag	10 Rowney Perfix
2 Correction fluid	fixative spray
3 Plywood and batten	11 Make-up brush
work tray	12 Old stippling brush
4 B pencil	13 Paper knife
5 Carbon pencil	14 Stanley blade
6 HB pencil	15 Dust-sheet
7 Giant-size	16 Cray-Pas
pastel sticks	oil pastels
8 White spirit	17 Cotton bud
9 Kitchen roll	18 Rowney kneadable
	putty rubber

Fig. 6 Materials and equipment for working in oil pastel, including a work tray to make yourself

a convenient place to put your other drawing equipment, such as your rubber, pencils and brushes. As your collection of oil pastels grows, you might find it helpful to lay out groups of the same colour family on the tray before you start working, grouping the most important colours, the three primaries, together. When you have completed your work, you can replace the pastels in their original order into their boxes, so that they are ready for your next project.

Cleaning oil pastels

Oil pastels do, of course, get knocked together in their boxes, particularly while you are working, so it is well worth giving your collection a clean every now and again. Cleaning the softest oil pastels is easily done by wiping them with a dry clean cloth or kitchen paper. For 'harder' oil pastels, dip your cloth in a small amount of white spirit or turpentine, wiping both the heads and the paper wrapper carefully. It will soon brighten up your collection. Nothing is more disappointing than a speck of the wrong colour smudging and ruining a pale passage in the picture. Therefore keeping the heads of the pastels clean is *very important*.

Keeping your work and work area clean

When using oil pastels for colour sketches or quick line work, you may find that a few unwanted particles of crayon work their way off the sticks onto the paper. By tilting your drawing at an angle and blowing lightly, you will enable the pieces to drop away easily. If they do not, I have found that flicking a soft make-up brush lightly across the paper removes these pieces quite efficiently without smudging the paper or light-coloured areas. However, now and again particles adhere firmly where you do not want them; on these areas, you can try either scraping the pieces away with a clean blade or, with a very small area, disguising the blemish with a touch of correction fluid.

Fig. 7 Still life of artist's materials worked in oil pastel

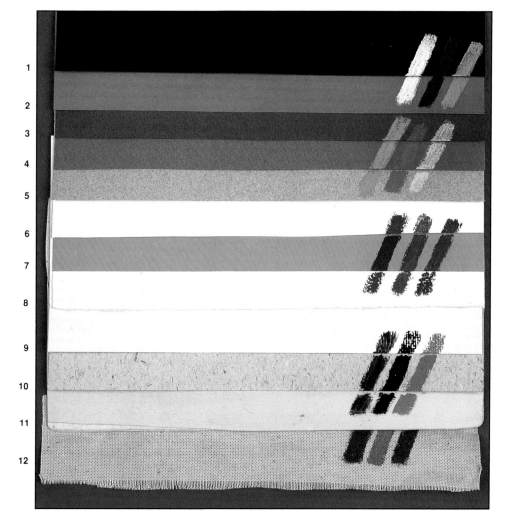

1 Canson Découpage bright-coloured
 tints, Black
2 Canson Découpage bright-coloured
 tints, Orange
3 Canson Mi-Teintes, Slate Blue
4 Canson Mi-Teintes, Beige
5 Canson Mi-Teintes, Slate Grey
6 Canson White paper
7 Canford Smooth Coloured paper
8 Saunders Waterford paper
9 Rowney Oil Painting paper
10 Packing cardboard
11 White soft wood
12 Canvas cloth

Fig. 8 Selection of supports
for oil pastel work

For indoor work, when you are using your pastels over large areas or using the engraving technique described on page 20, it is worthwhile, indeed almost essential, to have a dust-sheet or plastic protection on the floor to catch small pieces of pastel, as they stick to the floor or carpet as efficiently as they do to your drawing surface.

Pencils and brushes

If you want to sketch in your basic design before adding colours, use only an HB or harder graphite pencil. Pencils have a tendency to smudge and show through light-coloured work, so your pencil should be used as lightly and sparingly as possible. When I have done the preliminary drawing in pencil, I quite often rub out as much as I can, leaving just enough line work as a guide for the next stage. If, on the other hand, you want the effect of the graphite mixing with the oil pastel, use softer leads (1 to 6Bs) or work with carbon pencils.

You will need an old stiff hog brush if you want to use the stippling method of applying oil pastel. This is described in detail on page 20 in 'Basic Techniques and Exercises'. A stiff brush is also useful for the encaustic method described on page 21.

Supports

When using oil pastels by themselves, without paints or other media, you enjoy the great advantage of being able to work on almost any paper or card. **Fig. 8** shows a selection of supports suitable for oil pastel work. This 'dry' medium takes on almost any surface and does not stretch or buckle papers. However, the grain or finish of the support does have an effect on the work. A rough surface prevents you from obtaining a shiny finish and, unless you press the oil pastel down firmly to fill the dips in the paper, you will have a broken colour effect with the ground colour of the paper showing through. This can be considered an advantage, but only, of course, if this is the effect you want to achieve.

Before you start using oil pastels on a coloured ground, it is worth cutting a strip from the larger sheet to test how the individual colours respond to the toned paper. You will see examples of these effects on page 16 in 'Experimenting with Colour'.

11

Fig. 9 The basic essentials when working away from home

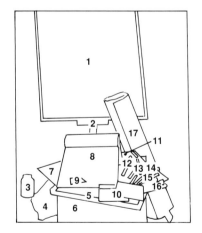

1 Painting on
   drawing board
2 Lightweight
   Warwick folding
   aluminium easel
3 Jar containing
   white spirit or
   turpentine
4 Clean rag
5 Work tray
6 Cardboard box
7 Sketchbook
8 Canson Mi-Teintes
   assorted colour
   sketchbook
9 Drawing rubber
10 Small box of
   oil pastels
11 Sketchbook with
   tissue paper
   interleaved
12 Waterproof pen
13 Watersoluble pen

14 HB pencil
15 B pencil
16 Bulldog clip
17 White and tinted paper

Boards and easels

I have found that a fairly firm plywood board provides a better base as a drawing board than a piece of hardboard which is often recommended for other artwork The hard shiny surface of hardboard is unsympathetic to any pastel work. The support needs just a little 'give'; this allows for a more sensitive handling of the pastel.

If you want to use an easel, you must give some thought to the scale of your work. If you think you will be doing large work, then your easel needs to be reasonably sturdy, but for smaller pictures for both indoor and outdoor painting, you should consider a lightweight sketching (portable) easel.

Working away from home

Whether you are going out for a day's sketching or embarking on a painting holiday, you will find it helpful to give some thought in advance to the equipment you

12

will need to take with you. **Fig. 9** shows the basic essentials. For colour work, a box of 12 or 24 oil pastels is plenty. If your local art supplier sells oil pastel sticks individually, an extra stick or two of white might be helpful; otherwise work within the range of colours that you have.

Other requirements for working away from home are: white and tinted paper (and/or a sketchbook with tissue paper interleaved); one HB and one 1B pencil; a good drawing rubber; one waterproof and one watersoluble pen; two bulldog clips to attach the paper to the drawing board; one small container of turpentine/white spirit; clear rag/kitchen roll; a work tray (which can be used as a drawing board if necessary); lightweight easel such as the Daler-Rowney Warwick folding aluminium easel; folding stool.

Working in mixed media

Oil pastel combines very well with other drawing and painting media including acrylics, gouache, coloured and Indian ink, charcoal and pencil (**fig. 10**). The possibilities for experimental work are extensive and I have given many examples of this in the chapter 'Mixed Media' on page 60.

Practical tips

- A fixative spray can be applied to oil pastels. Several light coats will help to fix your work and therefore make it less likely to smudge.

- When storing oil pastel pictures, you would be well advised to put a thin sheet of paper between each one to protect them.

- Never leave your oil pastel collection or oil pastel pictures near a radiator or in strong sunlight – the pastel will melt!

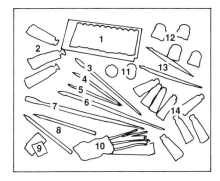

1 Watercolours
2 Acrylic colours
3 Watercolour
  brush No. 10
4 Watercolour
  brush No. 6
5 Watercolour
  brush No. 8
6 Hog oil painting
  brush No. 6
7 Hog oil painting
  brush No. 8
8 2B and B pencils
9 Rowney kneadable
  putty rubber
10 Charcoal – willow
11 Indian ink
12 Coloured inks
13 Pens
14 Gouache colours

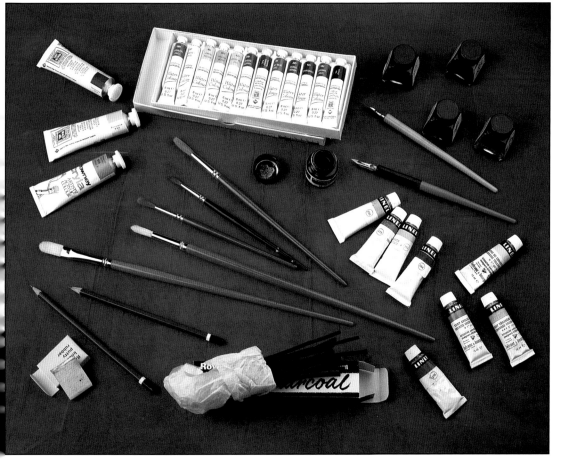

Fig. 10 Materials for working in mixed media

13

EXPERIMENTING WITH COLOUR

Bright, translucent, clear, vivid ... these are some of the adjectives that describe the quality of oil pastel colours. This is a lively set of words and, with others like sharp and dynamic, they suggest an energetic quality. The coloured sticks arranged in their boxes have a sharpness and brilliance that call for your immediate use. Unlike almost all other painting media oil pastels are generally used directly on to the support and do not necessarily rely on a medium for mixing. In the next chapter, 'Basic Techniques and Exercises', we talk about the different effects that you can obtain by using turpentine or other mixing agents and by blending the pastels, but at this stage I suggest you just try and discover the feel and effect of the colours used straight from the box without mixing them at all.

Colour contrasts

On this page and opposite, I have used the oil pastels unmixed to demonstrate some of the effects of applying the colours directly. In the abstract design which frames this page, the ovals are worked on white paper, allowing the colours to show their true value. I painted the surrounding area with a blue watercolour wash to add to the decorative effect.

In **fig. 11** I have combined a varied selection of random colours on each rectangle. Notice that the reds against the greens and the oranges against the blues present the brightest contrast. If you would like to try this exercise yourself, cut out smaller pieces of paper from a sheet of strong white cartridge or Canson paper. Taking your own random selection of three or four colours for each piece of paper, 'doodle' boldly, seeing if the groups of colours work well together.

Keep all this experimental colour work abstract, as I have done, resisting the temptation to draw specific objects, views or figurative images. Just revel in the pleasurable and surprising effects of the colours. You could vary this exercise by drawing bands of coloured stripes either diagonally or horizontally across the page, working from the palest to the darkest of your pastel collection. Experiment further with other combinations. For example, group the warm colours like the reds, yellows and oranges or, by contrast, use the colours that give a cool effect like those closer to the blues and greys. The pastel bands in **fig. 12** run from warm colours at the top to cool colours at the bottom. The possibilities are almost limitless. Don't forget that the purpose of experimenting with colours at this stage is simply to discover something of their potential, so leave descriptive work until later. However, if you feel really brave, work on large sheets of paper, as the larger your paper, the greater the challenge will be.

These first exercises calling for you to select colours and find out how they work together will help you to achieve a free approach to pictorial work. You will also begin to discover the differences between using oil pastels and more conventional artists' materials.

Colour studies

If you observe the colours in your surroundings, you will see that they change and move around as the light alters as though in the hands of a conjuror. But it is not only light changes that cause colour to behave differently from what one might expect. The relative coolness, warmth, strength, hue or tone will also change when one colour is placed on or against another.

Before I go on to give you some examples of these effects, I have listed below a few of the terms I have used to describe colours:

Hue The colour of an object or landscape determined by light and weather. Distant hills may appear purple in certain conditions, although the 'actual' colour is green.

Tone or tonal value This is the lightness or darkness of a colour.

Temperature This describes the warm or cool appearance of colour.

Local colour This is the 'actual' colour of an object uninfluenced by reflected light or colour.

All colour mixing begins with the three primary colours. These three colours form the basis of all the other colours. Countless hues can be made by mixing any two primaries in varying proportions. Introduce black and white into your mixing and you have an almost limitless range of colours. The colours which are described as secondaries are those which are made from any two of the primaries:

> Red + Yellow = Orange
> Blue + Yellow = Green
> Red + Blue   = Purple

Fig. 12

Fig. 11

Fig. 13 shows how the three primary colours appear to change their 'hue', 'tone' and 'temperature' when placed against different coloured grounds. The red dot shows up sharply against the white strip, but on the orange band it is evident how slight the contrast is between the two colours. On the grey, the red assumes a coolness contrasting with the warmer appearance of the same red on the brown. The yellow dot, as you would expect, 'shines' out brightly from the black but almost disappears on the cream. The blue dot, like the red and yellow, appears to change its colour value when set on different grounds. It is more 'blue' against the orange, but makes an altogether different statement on the slate grey strip.

Fig. 14 is another clear example of how colours which are constant in themselves can appear to change. The four differently coloured pastels drawn around this circle show how the ground tints affect their appearance. All four pastels are of the 'softer' waxier type and so have good covering power, and yet they all change their strengths from one coloured ground to another. If you are not sure which coloured ground to use, take small pieces of the different papers you are considering using and draw firm lines across them with a selection of your pastels. If you find that a yellow loses its bright 'yellowness' on a dark ground, whereas you want this pastel colour to maintain its full power in your picture, choose a light coloured paper such as white or cream. The light grounds generally heighten the lighter-coloured pastels. This is not always the case, so it is important to test the variations of colour for yourself before beginning a picture.

Fig. 15 is a further simple, but very effective example of the illusions created by setting one colour against another. It is important to realize that both pieces of white paper are from the same sheet, and yet how starkly the white shows up when set on a black ground in contrast to a soft grey ground. The paper on the grey ground appears almost off-white, giving an altogether softer effect. The power of the white paper on the black also tricks one into thinking that it might be slightly larger than the one on the grey.

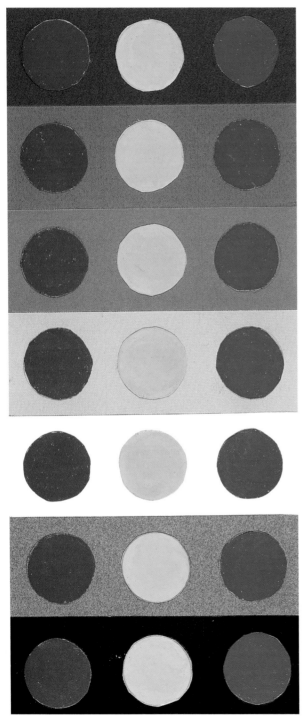

Fig. 13

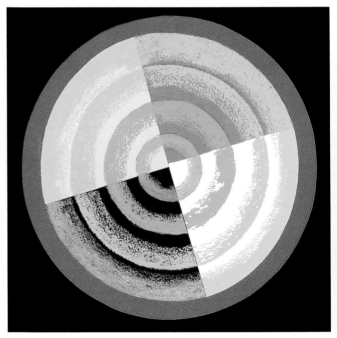

Fig. 14

Fig. 15

The colour wheel

Colour not only helps us to enrich a design; it can also be used to suggest a feeling of space, volume and movement. It also encourages different responses from both the artist and viewer.

Look at the range of tones from black to white around the colour wheel (**fig. 16**) and you will see that the bluish hues are darker in tone and that the yellows are lighter. In pictorial and design work, colours that are used close together on the page, but come from opposite sides of the spectrum, create forceful and vibrant work, while a visually more peaceful, quieter result is achieved by colours that are close to one another on the colour wheel.

Fig. 16 The colour wheel

Fig. 17 Landscape in summer

Figs. 17 and 19 are two examples of pictorial work which demonstrate the different effects achieved by using colours from all around the colour wheel or from just one section of it.

The picture in fig. 17 was drawn in summer, when the light was at its brightest and the contrasts were strongest. The picture shows red poppies jostling against bright greens, with warm yellows shining over the landscape casting purple shadows. This is an example of work where the colours were chosen from all around the spectrum in order to achieve a bold, bright effect with a range of strongly contrasting tones and both warm and cool hues.

Fig. 19 shows the same subject drawn in the autumn. The light is softer and so the contrasts are less marked. The predominant colours are reds, browns, and oranges – the colours of autumn. Because the colours are close to one another on the colour wheel, the visual impact is calmer.

The small abstract images in figs. 18 and 20 reflect the colours I used for the representational landscape pictures above them. It is worth mentioning here that, although there has been a lessening of interest in abstract painting since the 1980s, it certainly retains an important place in the tradition of the fine arts, and is, of course, still practised. So don't hesitate to put figurative work to one side if the notion of exploring shapes, spaces, lines, patterns and colours within an abstract

Fig. 18 Abstract in summer colours

18

Fig. 19 Landscape in autumn

context entertains you. In many ways oil pastels are an excellent medium for such work, whether it takes the free or 'expressionist' direction, or the premeditated planned approach.

Fig. 20 Abstract in autumn colours

Creating form or pattern is what we are mostly concerned with in picture-making. This means organizing the main shapes and areas of colour so that the picture balances well. The right selection of colours becomes very important with oil pastels. Remember that they are not mixed together in the same way as other artists' colours; your 'palette' is the paper on which you are working. This simplification of use from the subtle nuances and tones of other painting media sharpens up the work and makes it look bolder and more contemporary.

It has been said that 'to use colours beautifully, you must feel them, fall a bit in love with them', which is a nice idea, and in my opinion the most important twentieth century painter to increase our awareness and appreciation of colour was the French painter, Henri Matisse (1869–1954). Often pupils say to me, 'I am just longing to work more freely and break away from my usual style and colours.' Perhaps by following some of the exercises shown in this chapter and later chapters in the book, and by experimenting with the oil pastel shades, you will find that your general approach to colour selection will change and you will begin to see greater freedom in your work.

BASIC TECHNIQUES AND EXERCISES

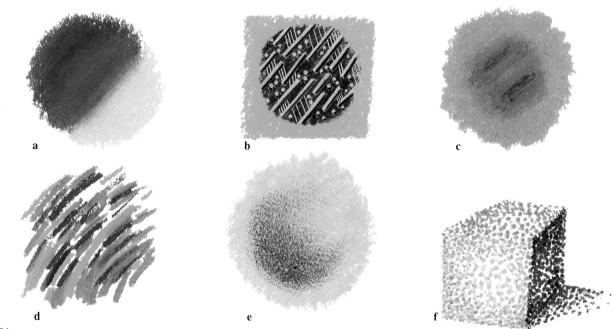

Fig. 21

In the previous chapter I talked about colour and how it behaves, and demonstrated something of its power and effect. Now it is time to explore some of the drawing methods you can use in order to have fun with colours. Oil pastel is a very versatile medium offering the possibility of a large range of styles and finishes. The examples in **figs. 21** and **22** show you some of the effects that can be obtained with the pastels by using various techniques. They are all drawn on white paper to show up the strokes more clearly. Try some of these exercises using your own colours. You can use white or coloured grounds and work on any scale.

Blending method (fig. 21a) Here is an example of two colours blended together. To achieve this result you will need quite a lot of wax on the paper, so apply a reasonable amount of pressure as you work. Now rub the colours together using your index finger. If you want smoother blending, rub with a piece of cloth dipped into a small amount of white spirit or turpentine. Use cotton buds for delicate work.

Engraving or scratching method (fig. 21b) Use a light tone for the base colour, working the pastel firmly over the paper to achieve a strong, opaque, 'solid' ground. When you apply the second coat, which must be darker in tone, work carefully so that the first coat

remains undisturbed. Now, with a pointed instrument such as scissors or a penknife, 'engrave' into the top coat to reveal the colour underneath. This method is particularly suitable for design and pattern work or for any image where line rather than mass is important.

Applied layers (fig. 21c) This example shows the effect of 'moving' the colour around by working vigorously over it with contrasting colours. I started with a marigold orange, then applied a coat of yellow ochre and finally worked in the dark green. This method can produce a soft, rich quality.

Linear method (fig. 21d) This patch of strong colours demonstrates in a bold way the application of pastel using broad flat strokes to create a sense of movement.

Stippling method (fig. 21e) As in the first two examples, you need to apply a good solid ground of colour to work over. You also need a stiff brush (a stippling or bristle brush as used for oil painting). Dip the brush into a solvent (turpentine or white spirit), then work it around on the tip of the pastel stick, collecting colour in much the same way as you pick up paint from a paint box. With your brush at right angles to the picture plane, dab the colour on. Do not press hard; if you do, you will end up with patches of solid colour rather than the open effect of stippling. This way of working creates depth and form whilst maintaining a light and sensitive feel to the work.

Pointillism or dot method (fig. 21f) Here the soft points of the pastels are worked to give an open effect to suggest light reflecting from an object. The white paper showing through the colours helps to enhance this luminosity and brightness.

Background work (fig. 22a) Finding a reasonably pointed edge on each pastel, build up a textured surface of different colours using line strokes only. The pastels need a clean edge to produce neat lines.

Hatching method (fig. 22b) This series of parallel lines hatched diagonally can be useful for shading or blending work. If your lines are close together, the colour mix will become quite dense because little white paper is showing. If your strokes are fairly open, the results will be lighter as the white paper plays a more important role. The 'edge' of the stick disappears rapidly as you work with it due to the softness of the wax, which means you have to move the stick around to find a new and crisper angle to draw with. If you have worked away all the angled edges, you will have to cut the stick to an appropriate shape with a sharp knife. The scale of your drawing determines how fine your lines need to be. For instance, if you are working on a large picture, even quite broad pastel strokes will appear relatively narrow.

Broad strokes (fig. 22c) Take off the paper wrapper and draw with the side of the pastel, applying pressure.

The width of the drawn bands is determined by the length of the stick.

Overlaying (fig. 22d) This effect results from simply dragging one colour over another, allowing as much colour as you wish to come through from each layer.

Bold strokes (fig. 22e) For large work use bold, broad strokes to achieve a quick and effective coverage of the paper. This is a useful method, particularly for trees, skies and water.

Broken textures (fig. 22f) By finding a clean edge on the pastel and then rotating it between your thumb and index finger as you apply it to the paper, you can achieve this rather wispy line.

The encaustic method

The effects shown in **figs. 23** and **24** are produced by the encaustic method. With this method you need a rigid support such as a board or paper glued to a board. The surface must not be pliable, otherwise you risk the wax cracking or breaking away from the surface. You will also need three or four coloured pastel sticks and heat-resistant containers in which to melt the oil pastels – a bun tin works well.

Cut the pastel sticks in half and place a piece of each colour into separate wells of the bun tin. Place the tin over a low heat. Take care not to burn your hands whilst doing this! It will only take a few moments for the wax to melt. Now scoop out some of the liquid wax with a palette knife and start working it on to the painting surface. You must work fast, as the wax is only pliable

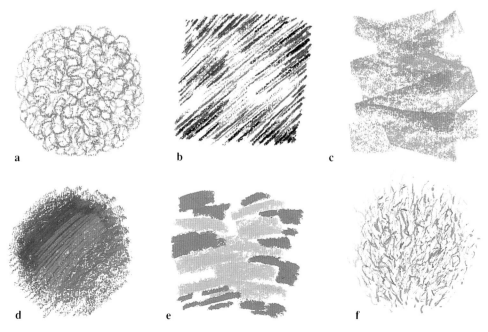

a   b   c

d   e   f

Fig. 22

Fig. 23

Fig. 24

while it remains warm. In this way you can build up a picture as in **fig. 23**. You can also use a stiff brush to work the colour. Alternatively, by dipping a piece of string or cord into the warm wax, you can convey the colours on to the painting surfaces to obtain effects as in **fig. 24**. For broader areas of colour you will have to find larger heat-resistant containers, such as empty food cans, to hold the increased quantities of wax.

This technique offers a variety of decorative possibilities which can be used in design and pictorial work. I would suggest that it is more suited to abstract work, until you have gained experience and have learned how to control the liquid medium.

Three jugs

The three jugs in **fig. 25** have been drawn employing three different approaches. The jug on the left is worked in areas of flat colour against a solid blue ground. The jug in the centre shows on its left-hand side a suggestion

of form, while on its right-hand side the introduction of reflected light begins to suggest more of a rounded form. This has been achieved by leaving areas of the paper blank so that the white shows through, but could equally well have been created by the engraving method shown in **fig. 21b**. The third jug has been drawn with both highlights and hatched shadows on it. On the background, the pastel has been used with light strokes at the top and densely at the bottom to represent cast shadows. This creates variations of tone – a more naturalistic treatment.

I have drawn these three jugs purely to illustrate how the same subject can appear quite different according to the method of applying the oil pastel. I make no claim to prefer one method to another, but let the exercise speak for itself. As you look at the illustrations throughout the book, you will recognize some of the methods described in this chapter. Most of the pictures demonstrate one method of working, but in some a combination of techniques is used.

Fig. 25

COMPOSING A PICTURE

When thinking about composing a picture, there are certain guide-lines and techniques that will help you to look at your subject matter more critically.

The Golden Section

For a long time artists adhered strictly to a set of rules, or proportions, called the Golden Section or the Golden Mean. This structure, thought to contain a hidden harmonic proportion, can almost always be found in work that balances well. Nowadays, however, artists often choose to move away from such clearly defined rules, seeking to challenge the eye and emotions with less restful proportions and giving greater emphasis to the impact of colour and texture.

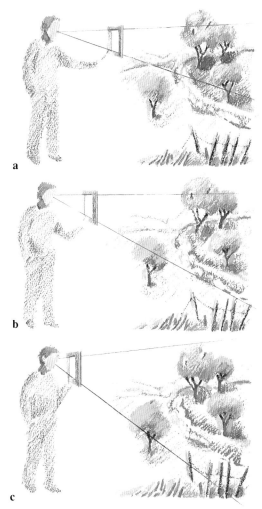

a

b

c

Fig. 26

Using a viewfinder

Most of us are reasonably familiar with looking through a camera lens. We select and 'frame' the subject of our choice, focusing on a chosen viewpoint. In effect we do this, too, when we focus on a subject for painting, whether it is an indoor or an outdoor subject.

The most popular way of selecting a subject is to use a viewfinder, which follows the same principle as a viewfinder in a camera. This can be a small frame made of light cardboard, approximately postcard size with the opening or aperture cut to comfortable proportions, for example 10 × 8 cm (4 × 3 in) or 8 × 6 cm (3 × 2½ in). For a horizontal 'landscape' view you will need to prepare a card with, I suggest, an opening of 10 × 6 cm (4 × 2½ in). The same card turned upright offers you a 'tall' view with the emphasis on the vertical.

First use your viewfinder with your arm outstretched, as in **fig. 26a**, moving it slowly around in front of the subject you are thinking of painting. Then hold the viewfinder closer to you (**fig. 26b**) and finally hold it even closer (**fig. 26c**), looking through the opening with one eye closed. You should be continually looking for groupings within the subject that you find stimulating. Often you will discover a composition that is quite different from the scene you first thought of painting. This might be a detail which can be transformed into a challenging or imaginative subject. So whether you want to produce a representational description of an interior, or a landscape, or perhaps even a still life, your priority lies in choosing a view which you feel balances well, with proportions that fit comfortably into the frame of your viewfinder.

Working from quick sketches

The approaches to composing a picture that I have described above are challenging and it is worth practising them to develop a more critical and observant eye. However, in order to approach a subject more freely, you may choose to work directly over a preliminary sketch which you have drawn without first using a viewfinder to compose the picture.

Select a group of objects or a view from your window and spend 10–20 minutes doing your drawings. It does not matter at this stage what you choose to draw, but keep these sketches small, not larger than a postcard. Then carry out the 'focusing' frame work that I have illustrated in **figs. 27–29**.

23

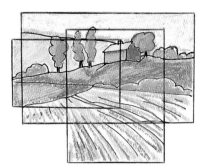

Fig. 27

Fig. 28

Fig. 29

I have drawn a distant view (**fig. 27**), a view through a window (**fig. 28**) and a bowl of fruit (**fig. 29**). Around each one of these I have described a series of rectangles and next to each of the drawings I have selected two of the possible 'framed pictures' and drawn them separately in black-and-white. This allows us to see the image more clearly and also defines the tonal balance. From these various framed images I am then able to extract the one that I feel works best compositionally and draw it out as the basis for a final composition.

In **fig. 30** I have again extended the 'field of vision' by drawing three extra rectangles over the original sketch, working 'out' from the original drawing where necessary and so completing the image. **Fig. 31** shows how I have drawn the three rectangles separately in colour as an aid to determining a final choice of subject. This is a very entertaining process and one that often suggests stronger, more interesting compositions than those that come naturally, unless you are very experienced in selecting arrangements of form and colour. This process is well worth using often. It is an exercise in which you can learn a great deal about the dynamics of composition.

The virtue of using these practical ways to help compose a picture is that it often results in more interesting work. It can also save you from the frustration of needing to restart a poorly composed drawing when you are already well into it.

Squaring up

Squaring up is a method for enlarging a drawing. It helps you to change the scale from small sketchbook drawings, such as the one shown in **fig. 32**, or from photographs, to larger images such as the drawing on the easel in **fig. 33**. By drawing a grid over the picture in your sketchbook and then drawing a larger grid on your paper, you can transfer your work accurately from one size to another. Many people prepare drawings and take supporting photographs in the summer months so that they have enough information to work from in the winter. A selection can be made from this collection of images, scaled up and transferred on to paper or board for the final studio painting.

I hope these different ways of tackling composition work are helpful and give you confidence. Some people prefer to approach their work without using any of the methods I have outlined, and when you become more experienced, you will find that much of it will come to you intuitively. I do not believe there are any rules in the field of art, except those which concern practical and technical matters, so the methods described should not restrict you since they are part of the creative process and should be interesting and stimulating in themselves.

Fig. 30

Fig. 31

Scale
1 square = 5 cm (2 in)
Picture image
25 x 20 cm (10 x 8 in)

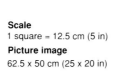

Scale
1 square = 12.5 cm (5 in)
Picture image
62.5 x 50 cm (25 x 20 in)

Fig. 33 The full-size
picture on the easel

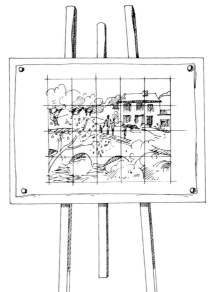

Fig. 32 Squaring up from a sketchbook drawing

25

FROM TRADITIONAL TO MODERN

Fig. 34 *Summer Fruits and Flowers*

Today's interest in painting is far wider than ever before. There is a huge and readily available market of art reproductions, enabling many more people to have access to them. The relative cheapness of reproductions, whether in print, poster or card form means that most homes now have one of more of these images on their walls or mantelpieces.

One of the influences of this influx of imagery into our homes is, without doubt, a broadening of our awareness and a greater appreciation of the many different ways in which subjects can be treated. This is enriching and can give us great pleasure; it can also be fun, and rarely lacks interest. However, this visual feast can, I think, be quite confusing for the artist, sometimes making it more difficult to choose the direction of his or her own work.

Flower paintings with different treatments

Let us take one area, always a popular one – that of flower painting. You will, perhaps, have seen a reproduction of a bouquet of flowers painted by one of the Dutch Masters of the seventeenth and eighteenth centuries, or received a postcard of a bunch of flowers painted by Monet or a flower print by Matisse. All chose to paint flowers, but their treatments of the subject were very different, as is the effect of their paintings upon us. Their styles may be classified as follows:

Traditional and descriptive The Dutch Masters' work was almost flawless with perfect detail of form and colour. They produced, without doubt, splendid and masterfully arranged pictures.

The painterly approach A Monet flower picture has a rich painted surface which stimulates our interest with its softly blended colours. I suspect that our affection for his work is, in part, a consequence of what could be described as a 'less than perfect' finish, compared to the painting of the Dutch Masters.

Into the twentieth century The bold flat shapes used by Matisse in his later pictures suggest light and sunshine, and look deceptively simple.

No doubt you recognize that there are a thousand and one other possible styles of painting to choose from, but within the context of the most commonly known traditions, these three span the most popular areas.

As an example of the many ways in which the same subject can be interpreted, I have treated the same image – a vase of flowers – in four different ways. I have used new colour groups for each picture in order to demonstrate the different moods that can be created while using the same imagery. Don't forget that I was in front of the same bunch of flowers each time.

With my first painting (**fig. 35**) I did not pre-select any of the colours before starting to draw. I had my full collection of oil pastels in front of me and took the colours that seemed appropriate at that moment to achieve a full and naturalistic description of the flowers. The work shows clearly that the light was falling from the left. Almost all of the colours have been worked in a direct way, using the tips of the pastels. Little or no blending was done. For this type of work you have to choose the correct tones quite carefully, selecting the lights and darks as accurately as you can. This image is fairly

26

Fig. 35

Fig. 36

naturalistic and is an attempt at a straightforward pictorial description of 'flowers in a vase'.

In the second picture (**fig. 36**) I chose a group of colours that worked well together, but were not colours related to the seen colours of the vase and flowers. I wanted to move away from the direct approach by working more freely and not attempting in any way to 'copy' the group in front of me.

I chose to work on the rough side of a white Canson paper. I worked the background of the painting with the side of a pastel, having removed the paper wrapper. Using a clean cotton rag, I dipped it into some turpentine and moistened it. I then gently dabbed the rag on to the orange background colour. This melted the pastel already applied, so that it spread softly and created a translucent effect, lighter in feel that the solid wax colour of the foreground.

I obtained the lightness on the roses and the cluster of pink flowers by using two methods. One was to apply the ground colour and then scratch some of it off with a

blade so that the white paper showed through. The second method was to blend different layers of colours together. For the reflection of the leaves and flowers I drew small patches of grey and orange. I would describe this work as free and experimental. The painting still retains a strong sense of form and space, yet is less naturalistic than the first example.

In **fig. 37** the same theme has been taken closer towards a flat decorative treatment. I introduced blue lines around the petals of the flowers to show up the distinctive patterns they make and continued putting lines around the white flowers and leaves. Instead of drawing the leaves as I saw them, I worked the pastel to form a patterned ground. I liked the effect and so decided to continue this patterning around the background area as well.

In **fig. 38** I kept the pastel work flat and unmixed, as if the blocks of colour had been cut and placed on the paper, making no attempt at spacial illusion – the result is more contemporary.

Fig. 37

Fig. 38

27

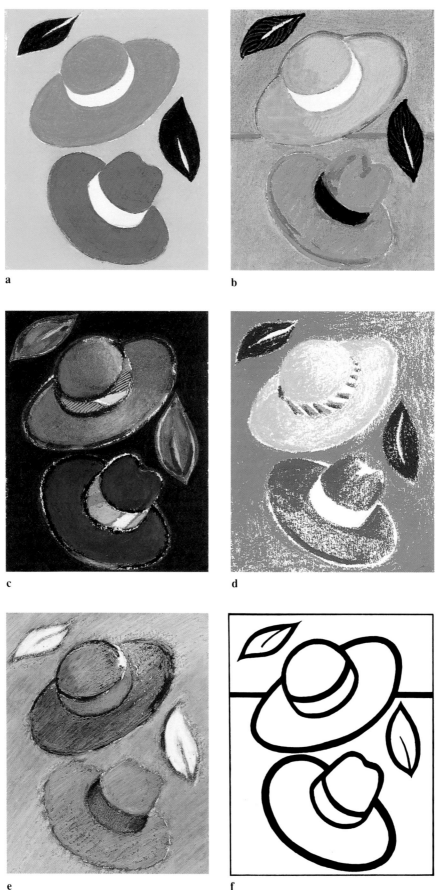

a

b

c

d

Fig. 39   e   f

28

Fig. 40

Fig. 41

Different approaches to pictorial work

Now that we have seen how colours can help to determine the mood of a picture and how spaces, shapes, lines and tones all have their emotional impact in pictorial work, we will emphasize some of these points by repeating a single image – a simple composition of hats and leaves.

A decorative approach (fig. 39a) Here the suggestion of form is slight, and the little there is comes from the perspective seen in the angle of the hats and leaves. The ground colour is a flat yellow and the four motifs are also worked in patches of flat colour, which is the principal element of this decorative treatment.

Creating depth (fig. 39b) You can see how a strong spacial quality has been achieved here. The warm orange areas come forward and the cool blues suggest receding areas.

Creating texture (fig. 39c) This example shows the use of a full range of colours, producing a broader effect. It not only tells us something about light and space but also suggests texture. This richer selection of colours gives us more information about the subject.

A cool and restful image (fig. 39d) This image lies quietly on the paper. The white of the paper shows throughout, helping to create the highlights and the feeling of space in the background. Tonally the colours are close and they blend together across the design without interruption, producing a restful mood.

A warmer image (fig. 39e) These colours have been worked to create a soft-edged look. The glowing pinks and oranges and the pale yellow leaves offer a sense of movement, light-hearted in feeling.

A simple outline (fig. 39f) The last picture shows the effect of simply outlining the motifs in black on white without any use of colour. It is clear and concise and produces a direct visual result.

Changing the viewpoint

Over the last few pages we have been looking at ways of altering an image, showing how a naturalistic representation can be developed into a picture with a modern feel. I achieved this by varying the colours and textures and gradually simplifying the forms, but I did not include any change of viewpoint or perspective. Most traditional work places the subject well within the 'frame', as in **fig. 40**, but the more contemporary approach often organizes the space within a frame differently. It reduces the field of vision and gives greater emphasis to the pattern element of the subject, moving away from the obvious to a more original and individual direction. **Fig. 41** illustrates how a detail of the French windows and shutters is treated in a contemporary way to make a bold statement and an interesting picture in its own right.

FOLLOWING NATURAL FORMS

Patterns from flowers

In the last chapter we discovered how a subject can be treated in a naturalistic way or simplified in form so that the picture takes on a more contemporary feel. Here we will follow the process of developing an image from its simplest outline shape through to an organized flat pattern. It is a thoroughly enjoyable exercise and frequently leads to unexpected results.

In **fig. 42a** I have indicated the simple outline shape of four different flowers – the sunflower, the rose, the lily and the sweet william. I drew them lightly with an HB pencil and then outlined them with a waterproof pen. The sunflower forms a flat disc, the rose fits well into a bowl shape, the lily takes a trumpet form and the sweet william, a multi-headed flower, forms a ball or globe.

Having considered the outline forms, you can now begin to draw the structure of the petals and colour the flowers, as in **fig. 42b**. I recognize that the fairly blunt shape of an oil pastel might make it seem an unlikely medium for work of this sort, but as you see, used carefully, it can be effective.

The third stage, shown in **fig. 42c**, is a small free drawing of the flowers in a natural grouping, as they might be seen in a field or garden.

Because of their size on the page of the book, the patterns in **figs. 43–46** look as though they were drawn on a small scale, but when you take a flower or leaf form to work into a repeat pattern, I suggest you plan it on to quite a large sheet of paper, for example 30 × 40 cm (12 × 16 in). This larger area will make it easier for you to develop a variety of textured patterns and permit the use

Fig. 42   a   b   c

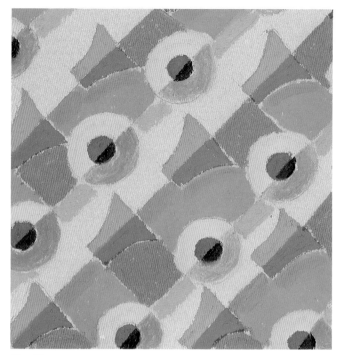

Fig. 43

Fig. 44

of an increased colour range. Using a tinted paper will influence the work and give it uniformity. The medium-toned paper gives greater value to both the light tones (the yellows and whites) and to the darker tones (the blacks and browns). These sets of colours lie at opposite ends of the tonal scale.

In preparation for the patterning work I drew a series of guide-lines across each square marked on the coloured paper, to help with positioning the repeated shapes. For each of the designs I went back to my original basic flower form: the disc in **fig. 43**, the bowl in **fig. 44**, the trumpet in **fig. 45** and the globe in **fig. 46**. My choice of colours for each of these pattern exercises was influenced by the natural colour of the flowers. However, by altering the colours, you can radically change the mood and emphasis of a pattern.

Fig. 45

Fig. 46

31

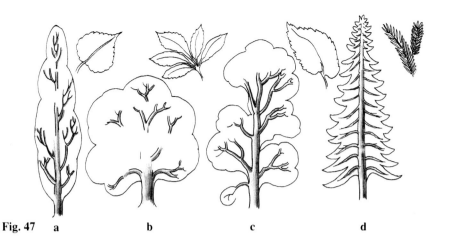

Fig. 47   a   b   c   d

Simplifying tree shapes

Between spring and autumn the leaf-covered trees are at their grandest and the fullness and variety of their shapes are seen at their best. It is during these spring and summer months that you are most likely to be painting outside, perhaps finding yourself overawed by the mass of different greens in the foliage. So here are a few notes and sketches to help you approach this subject. Before you start working, look for the general shapes of the trees, paying particular attention to their silhouettes. Where it is evident, note the basic structure of the branches; they are, after all, the skeleton of the tree and it is that which determines the form.

In **fig. 47a** you can see how the structure of the poplar, with its branches rising upwards from the main trunk at a close angle to it, forms a tall compact shape. The chestnut tree in **fig. 47b**, by contrast, is full and wide with large branches that spread outwards from the trunk. The elm tree is tall with a varied form, as shown in **fig. 47c**. The main trunk divides fairly evenly as it rises, and the smaller branches extend out so that the foliage creates sprout-like shapes. Tall and erect, the conifer in **fig. 47d** is rather majestic in its suggestion of symmetry.

In **fig. 48** the basic tree drawings have been coloured. This shows how the direction of the branches determines the shape of the leaf masses. In each of these coloured drawings you can see how various methods of applying the pastel have been used.

The poplar (**fig. 48a**) has cone-shaped groupings of leaves with gentle forms. For this I scratched away the top layer of pastel to reveal the pale tint beneath, creating highlights on the soft forms. The cluster of leaves on the chestnut tree (**fig. 48b**) are not unlike a series of

Fig. 48   a   b   c   d

Fig. 49

parasols with large rounded forms. I employed the engraving technique to suggest the candles on the tree, again scratching away some of the top coats to reveal the ligher colour. In **fig. 48c** I removed small areas of top colour with a blade to suggest the leaf pattern of the elm. In **fig. 48d** I only used one colour, a dark green, to colour the fir tree. To suggest the light on the foliage on the right-hand side I skimmed the surface of the paper with the crayon, allowing the white to show through, pressing harder where I wanted to suggest the form in shadow. On the left-hand side, I indicated detail with engraving.

Sometimes, when sketching, you might find yourself faced with a mass of hedges and trees merged together, possibly with the added complication of needing to suggest distance. Just remember, try and reduce the forms to their basic shapes, emphasizing the play of light and shadow. The light is at its best for this during the early or latter part of the day when the shadow contrasts are at their greatest. **Fig. 49** is a small quick sketch to show how trees and hedges in a landscape can be treated in this simplified manner.

Fig. 50 The colourful patterns of *Coleus blumei* leaves worked in gouache and oil pastel

33

SKETCHING

Fig. 51

Sketching is a very enjoyable activity and one that can be done both indoors and outdoors, in town or in the country. It requires very little equipment and practically no advance planning. You can move easily from subject to subject with no more than a pencil and pad in your hand. The slightest drawing can conjure up worlds. In a few strokes the smallest sketch can inform us about the time of day or the time of year, and give us some insight into the artist's life. After all, the artist is always behind the scene drawn.

Some time ago I came across a number of small sketch books, long since abandoned. They were amongst a group of paintings and drawings bought as a job lot in a sale. The sketches were not drawn by the hand of a particularly accomplished artist, and yet there were both moving and telling images of time spent and interest shown in many different things and places. Perhaps some of them had been used as reference for work done later. Each one could be said to have captured 'an instant arrested in eternity'.

Sketches are done for many reasons. Not least, they provide good practice in drawing skills, and encourage and develop observational powers. Although they are frequently drawn solely for the artist's pleasure, many

are valued as works of art in their own right. So never underestimate their value. Sketches often do play, and historically often have played, an important role for both the artist and the patron.

Approaches to sketching

Informative studies (fig. 51) Sketches of this kind are usually fairly small drawings, kept small for convenience. Their purpose is to provide information, not necessarily to give a pleasing image. So follow tradition and keep them small. In this way they can even be drawn on the back of an envelope or any scrap of paper you have to hand. The information you record will give you essential details like establishing points of scale, composition or lighting, all of which will be necessary when tackling a larger composition.

Tonal studies (fig. 52) If you want a tonal description of a scene, i.e., a record of the broad tonal masses, it is easier to work on a larger scale. Use one or a combination of these drawing media: 2B to 6B pencils, charcoal, ink, crayons or oil pastels. Using a combination of line and mass, you develop an illusion of volume and of light

Fig. 52

Fig. 53

and shade. When working, do not hesitate to smudge with your thumb or finger to create the softer passages. For more open areas of the drawing, hatching and cross hatching can be used to create subtle effects. By employing a range of different techniques, you can add variations of texture to your sketches to suggest changing contrasts and different moods.

Colour sketches As well as capturing the subject in front of you in black-and-white line or tone work, you may also want to record the colour in the scene. Colour swatches as shown in **fig. 53** will remind you of the hues in a landscape.

Alternatively, you might prefer to sketch directly with oil pastel, which can produce very lively results in

Fig. 54

colour. **Fig. 54** shows a working sketch that might be used as the basis for a studio painting. I would also want a line drawing giving more details of the foliage in the foreground before starting on a full-size picture.

The field of sunflowers set in front of a distant view was such a breath-taking sight that I stopped to do the sketch in **fig. 55**. I am often very busy in the summer months, so brief drawings like this one are useful reminders for later work. I tried as economically as possible to register the linear design and the tonal values in front of me.

Fig. 56 shows a speedy sketch of a 'figure in a landscape'. Even though the lines are minimal, there is enough information to work from. Try recording figures in a simple way like this as often as you can. It is a good discipline and forms a useful reference from which you can work on a later picture without having a model on the spot!

Here we have considered several possible approaches which you might find useful when sketching: the rapid informative drawing, the broader tonal description and the colour sketch. These approaches and the drawings which illustrate them are described primarily with outdoor work in mind. However, you can, of course, apply these techniques to working indoors, although generally speaking we most readily think of sketching as an outside activity. One of the reasons for this is that the sketch done indoors often turns into a drawing that we think of as a 'study'. The controlled comfort of working inside allows us more time and so we do not limit ourselves to putting down only essential information. Rather, we settle down to record the subject in front of us in a more considered and self-conscious manner.

Fig. 56

It is my experience that the more you sketch, the more information you tend to retain. Without consciously trying, you are building up a store of information which expresses itself later in your studio artwork. Often the slightest sketch will trigger off ideas of line and colour, reminding you, too, of the general atmosphere of the place in which you did the original drawings. Very encouraging!

Working away from home

There are many circumstances in which you might plan to do some painting and sketching further away from home, whether it is just a weekend break or short hotel visit, or a longer family holiday or organized painting

Fig. 55

Fig. 57

course with a tutor. Whichever of these situations applies to your next 'away from home' painting holiday, it is useful to plan in advance the materials and equipment you want to take.

If you are travelling by car, you have the advantage of being able to pack all the materials that you think you might need for your holiday work. This feels comforting because it gives you a broad selection to choose from when you arrive at your destination. On the other hand a small number of well-selected materials, often fewer than you think practical, helps you to develop the use of a medium more fully and to appreciate just how much line and colour work can be achieved with only a limited choice. I have outlined the basics that you are likely to find useful on pages 12–13 in 'What Equipment Do You Need?'

My feelings are that whether you are travelling by car or taking your drawing equipment as part of your hand luggage, it is beneficial to try to reduce it as much as possible. I often find that the most effective oil pastel

drawings or paintings have been done with a small range of colours. After all, the final results are rarely determined by your materials, but almost entirely by your ability to record your subject in a convincing way. I sometimes go out to draw taking no more than three or four pre-selected colours with me. This economical use of colour is helpful in simplifying work and is, generally speaking, a good discipline. I did the sketch in **fig. 57** using only four colours of oil pastel, but I have still achieved a range of depth and tone, and have captured the atmosphere of the country scene.

Working ideas

My impression is that most people do not go away on a painting holiday with any form of organized work schedule. Understandably, they hope that the change itself will stimulate ideas for pictures and mostly it does. Many of you will wish to leave your ideas for work open until you arrive, but for those of you who like to

St Juillard 8.30 am ~ a dazzling early morning shimmering light in the poplars ~ remember strong shadows ~

Fig. 58

have some structure, here are a few suggestions that you might consider interesting to develop for your 'holiday portfolio'.

Bearing in mind the huge influence the weather can play in this, you might choose to plan a combination of both indoor and outdoor work. If you only want to work outdoors and the weather does remain good, how fortunate you will be; however, should it break and you are obliged to work indoors, see that as an advantage.

Aim to produce one colour sketch in the morning and a second one in the course of the afternoon or the evening. If you are away for a week, you will have done 14 sketches, but over a fortnight you will have the impressive number of 28. By limiting the size of the work to not larger than 20 × 25 cm (8 × 10 in), you should find it easy to achieve the number I have suggested.

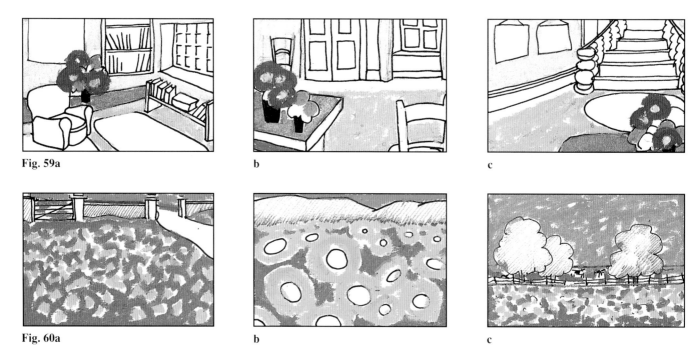

Fig. 59a   b   c

Fig. 60a   b   c

38

Fig. 61a

b

Diary Keep a drawn and written diary. This is descriptive work of the house or hotel you are staying in, perhaps including drawings of your room and other rooms inside the building, drawings and coloured work of the front and back of the building, and last but not least, the surrounding landscape. Leave a border around the work with extra space at the bottom of the page where you can write a few words either about the subject or your response to it. These notes, like the ones below the sketch in **fig. 58**, enhance your memory of the holiday and the place you have illustrated.

'Genre' pictures These are usually images which are small in size and depict scenes from everyday life, in this case, your 'everyday life' on holiday. The importance of the 'genre' picture is that it does not represent idealized life but simply things around you that you find interesting.

If you like flowers as a subject for painting, consider a series of oil pastel pictures set inside the house or hotel where you are staying, in which the importance of the interior is equal to that of the flowers. **Figs. 59a, b** and **c** give you ideas of different compositions with flowers and interiors viewed from various angles. **Figs. 60a, b** and **c** illustrate ideas for painting flowers out-of-doors, concentrating on landscapes in which the wild flowers are the most important element.

Another suggestion for a series of 'genre' pictures is to concentrate solely on interiors. Plan to describe a set number of studies of the interior of your hotel or holiday house in which the views are widely focused, giving as much information about the interior as you can. This means that you must be as far back from the subject as possible.

There is always a certain mystery in pictures of the outside as seen from inside a building, in other words, views through doors or windows. If you include some or all of the door or window frame, it indicates your position in relation to the subject. If you are far away from

the opening, your landscape will appear relatively small as in **fig. 61a**; the closer you are to the frame, the greater will be your field of vision as shown in **fig. 61b**. I am not sure why, but paintings that are seen 'from the inside to the outside' suggest a strong sense of the presence of the artist.

Supporting work All the suggestions I have given above describe specific ideas for sketching while on holiday. Whether you follow any of these or not, you might like to be reminded of the value of gathering information to take home with you. As well as line and colour studies, notes, photographs or found objects can be vital references for you when you are back at home, and are most encouraging and stimulating as you start to organize some of the holiday work that you did in the spring or summer, ready to develop into more considered winter paintings.

The most valuable references will be your colour notes, which should consist of drawn patches of colour with a written description of them. These colour patches are more likely to describe 'local' colour and your words to describe the more general feel of the day, i.e., grey misty day, lots of soft purple in the landscape etc. This sort of description can conjure up so much of the mood of the moment and help you to recapture the feelings which inspired you in the first place.

While the photographic image gives you an objective picture of reality from which you can certainly derive a considerable amount of information, only use it as an adjunct to your own studies and try not to rely on it too much. Unless you have a reasonable amount of experience, work done directly from photographs without other supporting references often produces a rather insensitive overall quality. Finally, if you gather a collection of natural objects such as grasses, barks, stones and perhaps a few pressed leaves and flowers to take home with you, it can stimulate a 'real' sense of the place you were in.

LANDSCAPE STUDIES

Painting outdoors, for all its known hazards and familiar discomforts, such as the day being too hot or too cold, or, as often happens, having to put up with the irritation of insects buzzing, still remains one of the most absorbing occupations. Quite recently I was working beneath a tree with drizzling rain falling beyond it and was not seated comfortably, yet despite these drawbacks I was so engrossed in recording the view that finally it was only the absence of light which forced me to stop, pack up and go home.

I might have begun by describing to you a painting session that took place on a light and sunny day, a day when there was nothing to interrupt the pleasure of working outdoors. As it is, I hope to encourage you to brave the elements as I did and to deal with any of the discomforts that you might encounter, realizing that often such a challenge stimulates a more concentrated approach, a more personal statement.

Most of us who set out to do landscape painting refer most readily for our inspiration to the works of Constable and Turner, to the Impressionists (both French and English), to pictures of the twentieth century and to the modern contemporary artists, in other words, the landscape paintings of the nineteenth and twentieth centuries. Most of this work was carried out with what we describe as traditional artists' colours. These are oil paints, watercolours and, less well recognized perhaps, gouache paints. But the second half of this century has seen a considerable increase in the materials available to artists. The most important contribution to painters has been the introduction of acrylic paints in the 1950s. Since that time there has been an influx of new types of drawing and colouring materials.

Amongst the most versatile of modern colours are oil pastels. Because of their relative newness as a medium, there is not a large collection of work readily available to which we can refer. Oil pastels are a modern medium and, as such, encourage a new approach, but we should not forget that the general rules of composition, choice of subject, colour and some of the techniques are the same as those considered important in traditional landscape painting.

Selecting a subject

I cannot emphasize strongly enough the value of selecting a subject as close to home as possible. You can spend too much time and waste valuable painting energy searching for the right subject to paint. If you feel uncertain about what to choose, put aside a morning or an afternoon in which to walk or drive around, slowly looking for painting subjects that you can go back to on another day. It is useful to have with you a small pad or sketchbook and a pencil, so that you can describe the place you have chosen and do one or two simple sketches of the views. I often note down two or three places of interest while I am out. If I am in a car, I mark the chosen spot on the map in pencil, because I find it all too easy to forget my exact location when my thoughts are concentrated on finding potential subject matter! Planning ahead like this means that you can consider ways of approaching the subject in advance.

Landscape techniques

Having found your subject, bear in mind the direction of the light, as you do not want to work with the light directly in your eyes. Think of your paintings or sketches as being either morning or afternoon pictures.

Fig. 62 Pencil sketch

Fig. 63 Colour sketch with pencil, first stage

Fig. 64 Colour sketch with pencil, finished stage

Working in one place for a full day can pose problems. This is because a radical change in the direction of the light changes both the colours and the shadows dramatically. The direction of the light plays a very important role in any direct descriptive work.

To demonstrate some of the working processes involved in using oil pastel for landscape work, I stayed close to my house in France and drew a view which is very familiar to me. It includes three rural buildings, two close by and the third set up on the hill in the middle distance. It was early autumn and the golden light of the sun, low in the sky, reflected its lovely warm rich colour on to the sunflower heads. The flowers, self-seeded after the summer crop, danced about at random across the fields. It was this feature that produced the initial stimulus. The rapidly changing season and the constantly changing weather make these autumn days, when the sun is still warm enough to sit outdoors comfortably, very precious indeed. It is a lovely time to be working outside trying to capture autumn's very special magic.

Pencil sketch (fig. 62) This is a sketch to establish the basic plan of the landscape, a very useful starting point before you rework your picture indoors. I drew it with a 2B pencil, shaded in the main forms of the trees and fields and described simply the three faces of each building in medium and light tones. I blocked in the

forms so that, when I came to work in colour, I already had a clear idea of the areas of light and dark.

You might consider that the buildings are the most important elements in the composition. But I particularly wanted the sunflowers to assert themselves, so I resisted drawing in their stems, and instead have drawn them suspended in space so that they appear to come forward to the front of the picture plane whilst at the same time relating to the field.

Colour sketch with pencil, first stage (fig. 63) Again working on white paper so that the pastel colours would remain soft and bright, I selected a limited range of hues which included light, medium and dark tones. I then blocked in the colours to define the pattern element of the composition.

Colour sketch with pencil, finished stage (fig. 64) This combines the drawing method shown in **fig. 62** with my preparatory blocking-in technique of **fig. 63**. In order to work over the pastel with pencil, I first used the blending method described on page 20 in 'Basic Techniques and Exercises'. I took a small piece of cloth, twisted it into a fine point and dipped it into white spirit. When you try this technique, do not let the cloth get too wet, just moisten it. Remember to use a clean face of the cloth for each colour and gently rub the pastel until it is smooth and silky. For the small patches of colour, areas

41

Fig. 65 Working on a tinted ground

Fig. 66 Working on a black ground

where I might have risked going across one of the adjoining colours, I used cotton buds, also dipped in white spirit. Used carefully, they are small enough to carry out delicate work.

Allowing time for the white spirit to evaporate and the wax to feel dry, I sharpened a 1B pencil ready for drawing over the pastel. The pencil work produces a soft grey-black colour over the pastel, thus giving greater depth to the picture. Using this medium in combination with the oil pastel is a very effective way of describing detail, line and shadow. It is also a very satisfying process to work across the silky surface of the rubbed-in pastel with a drawing pencil.

Working on a tinted ground (fig. 65) This example demonstrates the role that a tinted or coloured paper can play in colour work. I used a fairly bright yellowy-green paper which I thought would be a good foil to the blues. You can see how it has reduced the brightness of the yellows, but by contrast has definitely given the blues a stronger place. I left the green of the paper unworked over large areas of the picture, allowing it to assume its own colour role.

Working on a black ground (fig. 66) A complete contrast to **fig. 65**, this example has a strong dramatic quality with the black paper helping to enliven the colours. Working on black paper always adds a decisive, sharp quality, even though it frequently reduces the strength of the less opaque pastels.

Oil pastel with Indian ink

The last two small examples of landscape pictures demonstrate different methods of working solely with oil pastels. In a later chapter I will be taking you through various ways of introducing different media into your oil pastel work, a technique known as mixed media; in the meantime, here are three examples in which I develop the use of Indian ink with oil pastel specifically for landscape work. First I will describe in some detail the larger picture of the view from outside my studio that I painted for myself, before moving on to two more experimental landscape images.

View from Studio (fig. 67) I chose a full-size sheet of white Canson paper for this picture and worked on the

Fig. 67 *View from Studio*, oil pastel and Indian ink

smooth side. I indicated the main structure of the drawing using a soft watercolour brush dipped in diluted Indian ink. Whereas pencil sometimes smudges with the colours, waterproof ink will not, and this is one of its advantages.

To some extent your choice of medium for any initial drawing work should be determined by the final effect that you wish to achieve. If you do not want to risk any line work showing through, use a medium to hard pencil such as a B or HB, and draw lightly, finally rubbing away almost all of the pencil work and leaving just enough to guide you. If, on the other hand, you intend to cover all the basic drawing and have no line showing, an ink wash is perfect as it will not smudge. Yet another possibility is to leave the ink wash line apparent in parts, creating an interesting foil to the softer marks of the colours.

In areas of the painting where I wanted the sunlight to dominate – the hills in the background, the side faces of the buildings and the flowers in the foreground – I took the side of a medium yellow pastel, and worked it across the paper with broad flat strokes. Continuing the plan of working from lighter to darker colours, I selected a cool colour, a pale blue-green, as the foundation for the trees in the background and in the middle ground. I also used the blue-green pastel to work in open strokes across the field in the foreground. These open lines allow room for introducing other colours in the same area as the picture progresses.

I applied the darker colours, ultramarine blue (a warm red-blue) with purple, to help create strong shadows in the middle distance, using warm mid-brown to emphasize the roof lines and to add definition to the centres of the flowers.

Fig. 68 *Field with Sky*, oil pastel and Indian ink

In my small colour sketches in **figs. 65** and **66**, I coloured in the sky area. In my larger landscape the sky area is uncoloured with the white paper left showing. I often leave areas of paper 'empty', or free of colour, when I work with either oil pastels or gouache paints. The space left assumes its own importance, the white giving a crisp lightness to the coloured work. But there needs to be a comfortable balance between the worked and unworked areas, with well considered proportions; if not, the painting looks unfinished.

Field with Sky (**fig. 68**) This drawing shows a typical scene of a track leading from a shaded valley out into a well-lit distant field, with sky. I wanted to do a quick sketch showing the contrast between the dark and light areas as effectively as possible before moving on to a larger picture in oil pastel only. Basically it is a study of light and shade. If your time is limited, and mine was on this occasion, using an ink wash (as in **fig. 67**) to indicate the main areas in shadow is both economical and helpful. You are laying down an ink wash with variable tones which helps you to select the right tones for the colour overlay. Where the ink is at its blackest, you therefore choose your darkest toned pastel and, conversely, in the areas where the wash is at its lightest, you use your palest pastels.

If your original tonal work (ink wash) is correct, you have the choice of leaving areas of it uncoloured like in this example. If the colour overworking is tonally correct, the two methods combined should produce a harmonious result.

Fig. 69 *Village Scene*, oil pastel and Indian ink

Village Scene (**fig. 69**) In this last picture the use of Indian ink for the tree trunks assumes a very positive role, creating a striking effect against the oil pastel colours. The intense blackness of the ink acts well as a strong foil to the light receptive colours of the pastels. Both the ink work and the coloured pastel work have been used simply and directly, with no mixing of colours, to accentuate the interesting decorative forms of this quiet village scene.

PATTERNS IN THE LANDSCAPE

Fig. 70

The first time that I began to focus on pattern elements in the landscape was when I arrived in France to live in the middle of a wine-growing region and saw the vines in winter for the first time. From spring to autumn the leaf-covered vines form a wonderful patchwork across the countryside. It is a patchwork that changes its colours dramatically as the year progresses. In late spring the new leaves form a light reflective sea of shimmering green. Later, as the growth on the plants becomes fuller, the overall colour changes, until in autumn the different types of vines create a brilliant world of reds, yellows and greens, asserting themselves together under the bright sunlight.

I was so stunned by this stark patterning that I became aware of much to be enjoyed. Knowing that a pattern can be formed by a repetitive sequence of lines, shapes, colours or tonal differences and that this can also be created with purposeful strokes of a brush or pencil, or in our case the marks of the oil pastel, I began to see the full potential of exploring patterns out of doors. Much of it is the result of human design, like the perfectly measured vineyards, orchards or rows of poplars, but natural forms and structures also assume recurring patterns. Perhaps you can bring to mind the regular puff-

balls of cumulus clouds receding to the horizon in perfect formation, or envisage the natural movements and eddies in water making beautiful and well-organized shapes. These examples, and countless others, more than complement our own ordering of the landscape.

The most extreme examples of man-made features that create repeating motifs are those which extend across the countryside, relentlessly overcoming obstacles in their path. The largest of these are probably the giant pylons and telegraph poles, their wires often a favourite perch for birds. To these we might add the different types of fencing used to divide the land. A patterned surface, whether it is the work of nature or of human hands, speaks of a sense of constructive purpose, design and often exuberance. Including any of these features can give added interest and structure to a picture. So think twice before you reject them when planning your landscape work.

Patterns in the fields

I was out in the car marvelling at the autumn colours that had just begun to cover the countryside, when this pattern of fields (**fig. 70**) caught my eye. The summer

46

Fig. 71

Fig. 72

greens were still there, but some fields had already taken on the reds and golds of autumn. It was not a warm day. Threatening rain clouds raced across the sky and a cold wind was blowing. I was quite high up on a ridge over-looking this wide landscape and was keen to describe something of the crisscross patterning of the fields. Because the atmosphere was damp and the sun behind the clouds, the colours in the middle and far distance were soft and pale; only those close to me were bright and strong.

I selected a range of light colours for the background, reserving the strong colours for the foreground. The white of the paper helped to contribute to the pale effect of the distant colours. The fields furthest away, which showed the linear patterning, were drawn with simple, direct stokes. To define the details of the crops in the foreground you can see that I have used several different methods: the linear method, the blending method and the engraving method, mixing colours in all of these. The use of these methods brings out the richer colours and textures of the foreground and helps to give a sharper focus.

Continuing the search for strongly patterned forms, I stopped to draw these two quick colour sketches (**figs. 71** and **72**) one afternoon. In both I formalized the shapes and simplified the drawing and colours to emphasize the moving sinuous lines of the crops. I decided to rely on my own choice of palette (colour selection) in order to enhance the decorative quality of the landscape.

For the first sketch (**fig. 71**) I chose three basic colours – green, pink and blue. In the second sketch (**fig. 72**) I

again kept to three colours – this time orange, green and grey. The advantage of using a limited palette is that you can produce more decisive work that is often quicker to carry out. It is therefore a speedy and efficient way of selecting and putting down information to use for reference later.

Hay Bales The large round hay bales, which looked so incongruous in the countryside when they first appeared,

Fig. 73 *Hay Bales*, oil pastel and waterproof pen

47

are now seen as objects with considerable decorative possibilities and so are accepted by all with an artistic eye. Because of their large size, the bales are a dramatic element in the fields, emphatically defining the space they are in.

I roughly drew in the plan of the picture (**fig. 73**) with a black waterproof pen before starting to apply any oil pastel. Using the linear, hatching and engraving methods, and applied layers of pastel, I introduced colours which would suggest the strong contrast of light and shadow which these sculptural chunky blocks create. The stubble in the field, shining almost white in the distance, needed contrasting colours to show up well in the foreground. Because the sun was shining strongly, it seemed appropriate to use the Impressionists' palette of colours to describe the hay bales – bright yellow-orange on one face with the shadows drawn in the complementary colour of purple-blue. The distant woods, drawn in green and blue, kept to the same principle. I felt that there was enough descriptive colour work in this small statement to allow me to do a larger picture from it at a later stage.

Ploughed Fields In drawing, line is associated with motion. When following lines with our eyes we tend to endow them with movement, and it was the gently

Fig. 74 *Ploughed Field 1*

Fig. 75 *Ploughed Field 2*

Fig. 76 *Poplars and Wire Fencing*, oil pastel and acrylic

curving pattern of the ploughed field that made me stop to draw this view (**fig. 74**). I love the small shining chunks of soil that the plough blade forms as it turns the land into sharp furrows, reflecting the colour of the sky. I applied pressure to the lines in the foreground; as they receded, I gradually lightened my touch. I left the centre of the page clear to suggest light falling on that area of the field. Notice the scoring of the pastel in the foreground, and how the hedges have been kept simple in form by using limited tones.

The fields in **fig. 75** show a similar contrast in pattern between the heavily applied oil pastel in the foreground and the lightly drawn lines in the distance.

Poplars and Wire Fencing There is a strong element of patterning, too, in the picture in **fig. 76** with the regular vertical lines of the poplar trunks rising above the diamond shapes produced by the fencing. It is often simple scenes such as these in which you can find the most obvious patterns.

PEOPLE AND PLACES

Fig. 77

This title suggests both movement and stillness. We, as members of the public, are amongst those in movement when we are out in the town or country. As artists, our role changes. We become part of the stillness, observers sitting or standing and recording those around us. We are involved in sketching people moving about their daily activities, often set against a still background.

Begin by drawing in places you are familiar with, such as your home town or village. Then you will have broken the ground, as it were, before you find yourself in unfamiliar surroundings such as being on holiday. Drawing people for the first time, whether you are at home or away, is challenging. Many people put it off altogether because they are frightened of trying. However, even if you are inexperienced, perhaps never having attempted to draw people before, do try. I think you will be surprised to find that the slightest line drawn directly from life will suggest the movement and attitudes that people take.

Figures in painting

Having taken courage and begun to record people, however sketchily, you will find that it creates all sorts of possibilities in your pictorial and painting work. Landscapes, in particular, take on another dimension if there are one or several figures placed within them. The presence of people always adds enormous interest to any subject.

It is reassuring to look at the figure drawing work in the landscapes of some of the Impressionist painters, particularly those in which the figures are quite small and are part of an overall description of a scene. In these pictures you will see that often only a few primitive dashes, or blobs of paint, assume vigorously convincing descriptions of people, worked with a spirited spontaneity.

Recording figures

It is helpful to keep a small pocket-sized sketchbook to hand to jot down your drawings, and with it a soft 3B or 4B pencil. Using a very soft pencil or an oil pastel crayon helps you to keep your drawings simple, as they are soft and chunky and do not produce detail easily. Aim at first to draw in silhouette form, trying to create simple rapid statements which describe, however vaguely, the proportion and movement of figures. If you feel lost, not knowing at all how to begin, try and produce a few matchstick drawings and little by little 'clothe' them, adding more 'body' to them.

In **fig. 77** you can see how I have put down a number of figures in movement. Not one of them is drawn with any detail and each one is drawn in one colour only. I think you will agree that, however primitive the drawings are, they do represent quite convincingly the idea of people in various attitudes. They are drawn in a simple way, almost as matchstick figures. Try this method yourself if you are a beginner.

Fig. 78 shows how you can gradually add simple details to basic figures. Take an ochre or soft grey oil pastel to draw the entire figure and then dab on colour over the ground colour to describe the clothing, light and shade. As you see in these sketches, in none of them have I attempted to draw the face; it is quite unecessary for this type of work. As your experience and confidence develop, and if you find that you take to figure

Fig. 78

drawing, you might gradually discover methods of including detail such as hands and facial expression.

If initially you feel shy working out of doors in view of others, why not make a start by working from photographs just to get the feel of it. You can find endless sources to work from in newspapers, journals or magazines. These photographs provide a wonderful variety of poses. You will find images from static poses of people standing or sitting to people in action on the sports pages of newspapers (**fig. 79**).

Whatever your sources, speed is all-important, as working fast prevents you getting over-concerned with detail. Keeping the sketches small has various advantages. It is a controlling factor in the amount of time you can take to do the drawings. This is of great importance as even people resting on park benches tend to wake up and move away just as you have begun to draw them. If this happens, just move on to the next drawing! By keeping your sketches small, you can easily accommodate several studies of the same person in movement on

Fig. 79

Fig. 80 *Family on Beach*

Fig. 81 *Seated Figures*

a page, or describe quite large groups of people. Surprising though it may seem at first, you can fit all this on to a page measuring not more than 10 × 15 cm (4 × 6 in).

If you gradually collect your studies, you will have a source to use and refer to for composite pictorial work. I quite often put a figure into a picture even if no one was actually present at the time.

Recording the setting

A few strokes of pastel, however slight, can supply a great deal of information, giving a good idea of both the setting and the figures within. By indicating the setting you are also providing a scale, showing the figures in relation to their surroundings, as with the family scenes on these two pages.

It is worth bearing in mind that, simple though your descriptions of the figures might be, they need to be in proportion to each other and to the background. **Fig. 81** shows how the roughly sketched figures seated right in the foreground add depth and interest to the street scene behind them.

Fig. 82 *In the Park*

Fig. 83 *Family Picnic*

53

Fig. 84 *Walking in the Avenue*

Proportions of the figure

By dividing a body outline into eight equal parts, you have a useful grid to which you can refer (**fig. 85**). The head from crown to chin fits roughly eight times into the height of this figure. The hips are halfway down the body and are therefore placed at the centre of the eight parts. The length of the whole leg is approximately half the height of the figure. The hands reach about halfway down the upper leg, and the elbows are halfway up the arm.

These are ideal proportions, and you will soon realize as you start to sketch and look more critically at people around you that variations from this standard grid are very common. I would suggest that you draw one or two figures to establish these guide-lines in your head, but in no way be a slave to them when you are out and about working. That is the time to be as spontaneous as possible and to develop your own critical eye rather than working to a formula.

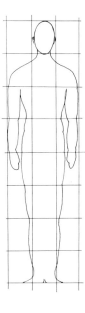

Fig. 85

WATER AND REFLECTIONS

Fig. 86 *Calm Waters*

Painting pictures either of seascapes or of the rushing waters of hillside streams has not been part of my experience in recent years. My home in France is well inland in an area where, on the whole, the summers are hot and dry and water is not plentiful. However, sometimes on these hot summer days the most rewarding place to be is by water.

Locally we have one or two rivers to choose from, whose waters flow more and more slowly as the dry summer progresses, yet whose banks offer cool and restful places to work. Closer to home, tucked quietly behind a mill, is the mill stream. These waters are always moving, continually agitated by the business of the domestic water fowl and other life. I talk in this chapter about some of the contrasts of painting the calm waters of a river in summer on one hand, and attempting to capture the colour and movement of busier waters on the other hand.

Calm Waters (fig. 86) Sitting by a river on a hot summer's day is a peaceful and tranquil experience. For us as painters, the only obvious change we have to con-

55

sider is likely to be caused by the sun as it moves around the sky. This movement gradually alters the shadows cast by its filtering rays. In planning your work, establish straight away where you want the areas of light and shadow to fall on the picture image. If you set out to work for a period of, perhaps, two to two-and-a-half hours, which is plenty of time to produce an adequate pictorial description, the changes that take place should not be too obvious in full summer.

If you want to achieve a strong, bright statement, a white ground is best. If you want to suggest a softer, quieter image, use a light- to middle-toned paper as I have done in this picture. In either case, draw in the plan of your picture with a pale blue or green pastel. Follow these simple lines by putting down any patches of sun-light in bright pale colours. To achieve this on a middle-toned paper, it sometimes helps to put a coat of white pastel across what will be the lightest areas of your picture. This gives you a light, reflective base for later colours: the pale pinks, yellows and others. These colours sometimes lose their light value when worked on anything but a white ground, as I described on page 16 of 'Experimenting with colour'.

Once you have established the basic structure of the picture, indicated the areas of light and shade, and finished the ground work, you can then develop your painting further. In general, my advice is to keep strictly to your original plan of light and shade. Do not be tempted to change it as you notice further differences in light occurring.

Fig. 87 *Movement by the Mill*

Fig. 88 *Vignette 1*

Fig. 89 *Vignette 2*

Movement by the Mill (fig. 87) Painting water in movement demands a good deal of concentration and energy. Last summer whilst I was sitting painting by the mill near my home, inspired by the bright excitement of the scene, I saw something swimming across the picture area, causing the water patterns to change completely – it was an otter. I was momentarily both amused and slightly irritated that yet another element had arrived, causing part of my subject – ducks on water – to scurry right of the scene. Fortunately it was not long before they were all back.

This activity, which caused the water patterns to change, is an example of rhythms altering as they often do on flowing water. It provoked me to rework some parts of the picture as I realized that, by doing so, the composition became more alive, more interesting. It takes courage to rework over already-established colours, but is almost always worth the risk.

All this observation demands vigorous attention, forcing you to remain alert. If you need a pause from painting the water, move on to the surrounding elements, such as the banks or trees or the distant views. When you feel refreshed and ready to continue painting the water, your eye and mind should be looking more critically at the essential marks you need in order to capture the right effect. If you do as I did and attempt to describe both water and the life on it, the same rules apply here as for general sketching: don't draw in too much detail, but keep to a simple statement that suggests the form and movement.

These settings in **figs. 86** and **87** describe very different water subjects. The first one is rather grand and still, with trees and surrounding landscape creating almost perfect reflections mirrored on to the surface. The second is primarily concerned with describing objects on the water, showing their reflections and the effects that their movements cause. Thus, the busy movement of the birds creates endless changing patterns, swirling lines and bright tips of light across the surface of the mill stream.

Vignettes (figs. 88 and **89)** To emphasize how effectively reflections on still water can be achieved with oil pastel, I have reproduced these two small colour pictures from photographs. Neither, you might feel, is a very unusual image, but at this point we are not concerned with the selection or direction of a particular subject, nor with its treatment, but rather with the practical ways of achieving the mirrored effect. Because the water in both pictures is relatively undisturbed, you can see how the forms and their colours are translated on to the water of the lakes almost perfectly, with no distortion. The only difference between the real objects and their reflections is that the reflected image will be a little softer and just a little lighter in tone. This principle applies to any subject mirrored on to water, including people, buildings and all natural objects.

If the water is really clear, it will usually reflect something of the colour of the sky and certainly will in areas where it is undisturbed by other reflections. Muddy water, water full of weed or water running over rocks or pebbles frequently maintains its own local colour, broken only by the change of light falling on to the moving surface.

The easiest and most effective way of giving an impression of water being a flat receding plane, in other words, showing the surface in perspective, is first to work the darker tones, i.e., the main body colours such as the blues, greens and browns; then draw a few horizontal lines across the surface in a lighter tone than the water colour. Gradually draw the horizontal lines closer together as they become more distant in the landscape. It always works!

Autumn Reflections When planning this picture I was not concerned with any clear direction of light. The day was hazy and the light filtered softly across the landscape. This was a scene which I loved for its contrasts. The rich colours of the autumn leaves were jewel-like as they floated still on the river, quietly sparkling against the softness of the surroundings.

Fig. 90

Sheltered by the side of the bridge, I did this first rapid sketch in ink with a waterproof pen (**fig. 90**). In it, the rounded shapes of the trees played an important role.

In **fig. 91** I then developed the same idea in colour. Looking at the second sketch I decided that I would give greater attention to the river and leaves. As I was looking at the water almost from above, I could see clearly the brilliantly coloured dots and dashes of the floating leaves.

To describe the leaves in the third and final picture (**fig. 92**), I used the oil pastel colours unmixed. I left the white of the paper apparent around the strokes to heighten the brightness. Because most of the water surface was covered by the leaves, the reflections from the opposite bank were seen only as broken patches.

Fig. 91

Fig. 92 *Autumn Reflections*

Fig. 93 *Bold Reflections*

You can see that the colouring is of my own choice and that in no part of the picture did I attempt to keep to the 'real' colours. I selected a group of colours that I hoped might best describe the rather lyrical feel of the scene. For a picture to work, to describe depth and form, it is only the correct use of tone that is vital.

Fig. 93 shows a river scene similar to that in **fig. 92**, but here I decided to focus on the water in the foreground even more closely. I used broad strokes of oil pastel which convey the impression of sunlight sparkling on the slightly ruffled surface of the water. Again, the colours are a very personal choice.

MIXED MEDIA

In this chapter we are going to explore different ways of working by mixing oil pastels together with other painting and drawing media. The term 'mixed media' can be used to cover almost unlimited combinations of materials. Indeed, if you consider some of the early religious devotional objects, it even includes the use of coloured glass, precious metals and stones. In the twentieth century all kinds of things, found or manufactured, have been and still are employed together with conventional artist's materials to organize effective images. These images, by their daring, break down formal barriers and attitudes and open the way for all types of experimental pictorial work.

The examples shown in this chapter are limited to combining oil pastels with water-based paints, inks, pencil and charcoal. As an introduction to 'mixed media', these materials offer extensive possibilities. When you have explored some of the effects that can be achieved by using these familiar media, do not hesitate to move on to more experimental work.

Six examples of mixed media work

Acrylic and oil pastel (fig. 94a) Acrylic paint dries quickly and, when dry, remains fast on the page. It produces an impervious plastic film, giving a perfect base for further work. Oil pastels take to it beautifully.

On the left-hand side of the motif, I have used the dot method for the background. On the right-hand side I have illustrated the scumbling technique where the pastel is dragged over the acrylic, allowing some of the paint to show through.

Gouache and oil pastel (fig. 94b) These two media also work well together. On the left-hand side of this image I first applied thick dabs of gouache paint, then added short strokes of oil pastel. On the right-hand side, the ochre, blue and brown are all worked in oil pastel, on top of which I painted a fairly dry mixture of gouache. The flat quality of the gouache contrasts with the richness of the oil pastel.

a

b

c

e

d

f

Fig. 94 Six examples of mixed media work

a Acrylic and oil pastel
b Gouache and oil pastel

c Pencil and oil pastel
d Coloured ink and oil pastel

e Indian ink and oil pastel
f Charcoal and oil pastel

Fig. 95 First stage

Fig. 96 Second stage

Fig. 97 Third stage

Fig. 98 Finished stage, *Landscape*, pencil, watercolour and oil pastel

Pencil and oil pastel (fig. 94c) This motif is drawn with a 4B pencil. To echo the found forms of the berries, I used a soft putty rubber (this malleable rubber is very useful for pencil and charcoal work) to remove some of the pencil on the left-hand background to form the white dots. To achieve the contrast of tone on the predominantly pink side, I used a cotton bud dipped in turpentine and took away some of the background colour. The black tonal and line work is in pencil.

Coloured ink and oil pastel (fig. 94d) I drew round the leaves and berries lightly and then applied a pink wash over the background on the left-hand side and also to the leaves on the right. When that was thoroughly dry, I applied a soft yellow-green pastel to the left-hand leaves and scratched over them with a blade to give the right variation of tone. I worked in the same way on the right-hand side, using a dark green pastel and removing some of the colour where necessary with both a blade and a cotton bud dipped in turpentine.

Indian ink and oil pastel (fig. 94e) The left-hand side of the background shows finely hatched lines drawn in with a fine drawing pen and partially worked over with a blue pastel. Ink also settles quite well on top of the colour. This is evident on both the background and the blue leaves. To get the rather vigorous markings on the other half of the design, I drew with a pointed piece of wood dipped in the ink.

Charcoal and oil pastel (fig. 94f) This combination is a complete contrast to the previous examples, having an altogether softer and gentler quality to it. I began by scumbling yellow pastel on the left-hand side, then charcoal on the right-hand side, varying the pressure to create different shades of black. I drew in the leaves on the left in black charcoal, applying even pressure. The leaves on the right were worked in with the same yellow pastel. I then scratched away part of the yellow leaves to create a paler effect. Finally I drew short vertical strokes on both sides with a pale grey oil pastel.

Landscape in mixed media

These small drawings in **figs. 95–98** demonstrate four stages of building up a picture, from a pencil line drawing to the finished colour work. You will see that the work progresses from pencil lines to a completed picture using several different media – pencil, watercolour and oil pastels.

First stage: Pencil (fig. 95) The purpose of this first stage was simply to map out the composition, to describe the small block shapes of the buildings and to indicate the trees and vines around them. The light shading strokes were marked to suggest the main shadow areas. This line work was done with a 2B pencil which is soft enough to vary the quality of the line without being too strong.

Fig. 99 First stage

Fig. 100 Second stage

Second stage: Pencil and first watercolour wash (fig. 96) The areas that were free of pencil shading I left ready for the watercolour. The wash consisted of light Lemon Yellow and Cadmium Yellow, brushed on these areas to show the sunlight falling across the landscape.

Third stage: Pencil and second watercolour wash (fig. 97) In this next stage I introduced diluted Cobalt Blue watercolour over the areas in shadow. Continuing with watercolour, I mixed Cobalt Blue and Permanent Magenta together to make a soft purple and applied the wash right across the sky. While the paint was still wet, I took a small piece of clean cloth and dapped out a patch of colour to suggest the cloud.

When you are trying to depict a landscape bathed in sunlight, experiment and try painting the sky much darker than it looks. I know that some people resist the idea, because they are determined to copy as faithfully as they can the subject in front of them. It is quite true that when the sun is shining, more often than not the sky appears to be blue, sometimes quite a soft pale blue. But if you defy reality and paint the sky several tones darker than it appears, it will give greater contrast to the other colours in the picture. All the pale colours, the yellows in particular, will stand out more clearly and the darker colours will look richer. Or you might choose to work on a mid-toned paper, in which case the sky will be darker to start with.

Finished stage: Pencil, watercolour washes and oil pastel (fig. 98) The moment had now come to work over some parts of the colour washes, using a limited selection of oil pastels. (Do be sure that any watercolour groundwork is thoroughly dry before beginning to apply other media over it.) The watercolour ground colours have a light, clear quality in sharp contrast to the richer, glossier surface of the pastels.

If you are working on a fairly small scale, as I have done for this step-by-step exercise, you will, of necessity, be limited to using a restrained range of colours. So establish which three colours are going to represent your three most important tones – the light, the middle and the dark tones. My choices for these three, as you can see, were a pale yellow, a mid green and a dark purple. The use of three tones with the light and shading already painted in with watercolour should certainly be enough to produce a clear tonal statement. Any other colours I have used are there simply to enrich the colour effect.

The rather crisp contrast between the light, translucent watercolour and the rich, opaque colours of the oil pastels suggested to me that further definition might add to the overall brightness of the image. To do this I outlined some of the details of the landscape with the same 2B pencil that I used to do the original drawing. (You will discover that ordinary drawing pencils soften when combined with oil pastels, often making the lines appear blacker than normal.)

Fig. 101 Third stage, *Fruit and Berries*, watercolour, oil pastel and Indian ink

Fruit and Berries

This picture shows a few familiar objects placed together and I have reproduced my work in stages in order for you to follow the sequence that I have taken. I suggest that you arrange a similar group and follow through the three stages, basing your work on my approach. If you complete the series to its final stage and are feeling confident, you might want to continue working on it. You could do this by either continuing with the watercolour, oil pastel and Indian ink as I have done, or possibly combining them with some of the other media described and used in this chapter. These are the first three stages; the fourth is open to you.

First stage (fig. 99) To establish the composition, I drew in the subject with brush and watercolour.

Second stage (fig. 100) I then worked over the watercolour in oil pastel and created a patterned background.

Third stage (fig. 101) At this point I strengthened the pastel work and applied Indian ink with a brush for outlines and darker tones. The painting can now be developed further if you choose to experiment.

Landscape study in gouache and oil pastel

In contrast to the rather linear, illustrative quality of the step-by-step landscape sequence on page 61, this next landscape (**fig. 102**) is worked more freely with a fuller use of paint and pastel together – a more painterly approach. I began by painting, fairly boldly, a description of the various elements of the composition with gouache paints. This is a method I quite frequently employ as a foundation for both oil pastel and soft pastel work. It is less committing than starting straight off with pastels. If you keep the paint thin and light in colour at this stage, you can alter the emphasis and balance of the picture easily.

Only start using the oil pastels when you are confident that the feel of the composition is right. As the picture progresses, decide how much of the paintwork you want to cover up. Sometimes you end up by covering all the groundwork, while at other times the value of leaving areas free of pastel is evident. Whichever way you think it might go, keep the paintwork loose at this stage.

Because so much of the white paper was covered by paint, I worked fast, using bold gestural strokes in oil pastel. In some places I reworked layer upon layer of gouache and oil pastel until I liked the colouring. If you layer your colour like this, with gouache followed by pastel, then more gouache layered over the pastel etc., you can achieve exciting and vibrant patches of colour.

Fig. 102 *Summer Scene*, gouache and oil pastel

These two media combine well, so that you can build up the layers until you feel satisfied with the results.

For example, the flower heads of the marguerites covering the foreground were originally painted as patches of white gouache. The centres of the flowers were then described with a yellow oil pastel. The trees in the background were also first painted with gouache, and then overworked with greens and blues in pastel. Right across the picture, therefore, from the top of the sky down to the marguerites at the front, the surface changes from pure gouache to fairly solid areas of oil pastel which are especially evident in the blues and greys of the sky, on the house and in the darker colours of the trees and hedges alongside the house.

We have now covered some of the methods that can be used when mixing different drawing and painting materials together. As I stressed at the beginning of the chapter, the possibilities of working in mixed media are extensive and this is no more than an introduction. It is now for you to experiment and develop your own work.